BONES

Janette Voski

Bones Copyright © Janette Voski, 2021.
First published on 5 September 2019.
This version was published on 5 September 2021.

All rights reserved. No part of this book may be reproduced or transmitted in any form or by any means without written permission from the author.

ISBN: 978-0-6485925-8-7

Cover image: Self-portrait, Janette Voski.

Also by Janette Voski

X

For the one who
over-thinks, over-analyses
loves with every atom they possess
feels everything deeply
has a broken heart, but is looking to find their way again
has a heart thirsty for love and adventure
found their strength prevails through pain

Contents

PREFACE • 1

BEFORE THE END • 3
Undeveloped
Your Father
Just Two Kids
Jeweller
Perfect
Fractured
Crazy
Unknown Sender
Deep
The Revolver

AFTERMATH • 15
Waterfall
White Wine
I'll Miss You
Winter
Don't
Seeds
A Moment
Ouch
Wanted
A Dance Duet
New Life
Green Eyes

CRUSH • 29
Punch
Thief
Thirty-Four Days
Promises
Wonder
Grief
Pain
Forever
I'm Okay
Permanent
Alone

Contents

SURVIVE • 43
Peace
Time
Relieved
Thanks for the Memory
The Little Things
Steam
Expired
Rock
You
The Pacific
Dear Diary

REALISE • 55
Thank You
One Day
Heartbeat
Reflection
Symmetry
Arizona
Wind
Wet
Feel

CONQUER • 65
Indifferent
Classic
The Next
Now
Heavy
1965
Roll
I Wish
How
Jesus Christ
Trigger
Developed

EPILOGUE • 79

PREFACE

Bones.

Because this book is like my body, and each page like a piece of myself. Written from the memories of every deep and dark corner of my mind that has been in hiding for too long. Scribbled into a journal or typed out impulsively in fear of forgetting. Musings turned into poetry and prose, exhausting the fifty-four bones in my hands alone.

Because this book is filled with every fleshy, bloody, dirty wound I have ripped apart and dissected for you to peer into, and all that is left is my bones. The very bones that were broken, that over time knitted together to form new bones.

Because I've healed.

Because I'm stronger.

BEFORE THE END

If only he came with a warning label
I still wouldn't have listened.

Undeveloped

Film must not be exposed to light.
It's developed in a dark room, until the time is right.

I stopped taking photos on film because I was afraid of reaching the end of that roll. Unsure if I could bear the thought of seeing you again, even if it would just allow me a memory from one of those days.

I still haven't and,
I'm not sure I ever will finish that roll.

So perhaps I will do what you must to film:
Develop myself in the dark
Until it's time to be seen in the light.

Your Father

He was kind and gentle.
His eyes spoke the words he did not.

His parents too, were kind and gentle.
Their love was exemplary.

When I told you I loved them,
I meant I pictured our life like theirs.

I don't think you understood.

As you were cooking, I wrapped my arms around your waist,
Rested my head on your back.

Your father looked at me and without a word
He understood.

Just Two Kids

We held hands every time we were with one another,
So much so, your parents asked, "Do you detach?"

I loosened my grasp between your fingers
You grabbed mine even tighter.

I couldn't help but laugh

They couldn't either.

Jeweller

We went to the jeweller
They called me your fiancée
My cheeks, masked with rubies
You smiled at me, wide and full of pearls
With emerald in your eyes, and
Gold in your heart.

BONES

Perfect

He was the perfect height for me, and I for him.

His lips reached my forehead
And whenever I hugged him,
I could hear his heart beat.

Fractured

Enough.
Either want me and show me you want me or leave.

I am not here to love you with the whole of my existence,
Only to feel a fraction of yours.

Crazy

How do you expect me to be when I am madly in love with you? I cannot be *madly* in love and simply not react.

When I say I am *madly* in love with you
It means you will feel all of me, love all of you.

You cannot tame my emotions
Because you are what is in my heart
And my heart is wild.

So if I feel my heart rip apart I will cry, and carry on
Because the thought of losing you is driving me insane.

And you call me crazy.

But if I weren't crazy, it would mean that I do not care.
For I cannot act rationally, when my love for you is already beyond reasonable measure.

BONES

Unknown Sender

I don't deserve to feel like I'm unloved by a partner who would rather see everyone else before spending time with me.

> When would I have the time?

That answers everything.

> So

So, you don't have time for me.
When you don't have time for something, what happens to it?

I don't remember what came after that, but I remember what I wanted to say:
It's like having a car with a battery that keeps dying. The ignition just won't catch. I keep trying to start it and start it, and when it does, the fuel just runs out.

So, I must get out and abandon you.

The thing I wanted to say the most, was:
I have a 54-year-old car, and I make time to maintain it.

Maybe that's why it still drives.

Maybe that's why it has lasted.

Deep

It is sad when two people share a connection
As deep as the depths of the earth
Just to have time pass
Where one continues to feel it intensely and irrevocably
And the other feels like it is slowly fading away.

The Revolver

Like Russian Roulette, a one-in-six chance of being shot
Only he was the one with the revolver
And it was aimed at my heart.

Eyes squeezed shut every time he pulled the trigger
Aim and fire
Aim and fire

I would try to move from his aim
But he kept pulling the trigger

Aim and fire
Aim and fire …

Aim and fire.

Finally, I took the revolver from him.

Aim and fire.

AFTERMATH

Is there beauty in destruction?

Waterfall

It was like we were the river
Flowing together and never drifting apart
Continuously keeping another afloat
Until the water began rising.

I tried to hold on, but I started drowning.

When the tides ripped us apart, I got cut from all the coarse rocks. My way down felt like I was caught in an endless waterfall. I was gasping for air.

I ended up at the bottom
I wasn't sure where to go from there.

White Wine

I was slowly sipping my glass of white wine.

White wine.
That's exactly what it was like, you and me.

It was so sweet, fragrant and rich in flavour.
But after a while, if you keep it too long …
It turns to vinegar.

All the sweetness was gone whenever I reached for a taste.

I'll Miss You

I remember the last words I ever said to you:
"I'll miss you."

I remember the way I said it.
My voice almost broke, and I covered my mouth with my left palm in fear of allowing you to hear my uneven breath.

For as long as we knew each other, I hoped you knew me better than that.
Fight for me.
Tell me this is not the end.
Tell me: I love you.
        Come back.
        Wait!
        This is wrong.
        I was wrong, you're wrong.

Please.

Say anything and I swear I'll turn this car around faster than these thoughts are running through my head.

...

"I'll miss you too."

BONES

Winter

A day after it ended, I woke up shivering.

I reached for my chest and tugged at my clothes, hoping the cotton would rip apart just the way I felt I was.

Anything, I thought, would be easier, better than this.
Should I go back?

I cried, the kind you could not hear.
Just an intermittent gasp for air and a silent mime of disbelief.

Months went by.
It's strange – feeling your heart breaking. Feeling your heart become as cold as the Arctic.

Feeling it become hard, empty.

I sat in the sun and felt myself shiver, skin riddled with goosebumps. The cold spread everywhere, like a disease. Breathing became sharper, faster.

It was 37 degrees, and it was Summer.
But there were the winds of Winter in my lungs and icebergs running through my veins.

BONES

Don't

After five and a half years of building our home,
I found a gas leak.
Slowly seeping into every room of what we'd built.

By the time I realised, it was too late.
One wrong move and it would collapse and burn.

Don't ignite it.
I whispered into his ears.

Don't ignite it.
I tried to air out the rooms,
Striding carefully, speaking softly …

Don't ignite it!
I cried it out

The flame was blue.

I blinked, and the rooms were engulfed in yellow and orange.

Suddenly I couldn't breathe.
Everything we had built together burnt to a crisp.

I inhaled some of the ashes and smoke.
They burnt the parts of me that cried out your name.

Seeds

I was just a sunflower.

"One day, I want to plant my seeds," I said.

When he left at dusk I began to wilt.

There was another world of darkness waiting
Beneath the moonlight.

When my stem becomes stronger,
I will find somewhere else to plant myself.

Somewhere with deeper roots.

A Moment

Everyone was applauding, they were all watching you
But your eyes were fixed on me.
When our eyes met, you smiled and winked.

I remember being so overwhelmed with surprise and joy that
my eyes welled up
I swear I felt like I was the only one in the room.

Maybe for a moment I was, to you.

BONES

Ouch

I gaze at you.
        "What are you looking at!"
The love of my life, I thought.

You gaze at her,
Your eyes astray.

You used to look at me that way.

Wanted

I wanted to kiss you wherever it hurt, because it hurt me too
I wanted to kiss you anywhere, at any time
I wanted to see you chase your dreams
I wanted to watch you walk away, only to watch you walk back
I wanted to close my eyes and hear you smile when you spoke
I wanted to console you through your challenges
I wanted to share all my meals with you
I wanted to one day share vows with you
I wanted to start a family with you, grow old with you
I wanted to give you everything you wanted
I wanted you to want these with me too

Most of all,
I just wanted *you*.

A Dance Duet

It was like a 'grand pas de deux'.

The entrée:
We met, and fell in love
A romantic and a beautiful love story.

The adagio:
We did pirouettes,
Sometimes we stumbled
Though always gracefully supporting each other.

The variation:
You turned and leapt in your solo
I fell in mine.

The coda:
The finale.
I cried, then the curtains closed.

New Life

You asked me to come back to help start your car. When I got there, I thought you would have said something else apart from "my car isn't starting".

I turned your car the other way while you pushed it
And I finally pulled up the handbrake.

You jet-setted off, seemingly no longer in strife.

It kills me to know you called me back
Just to help you start your new life.

Green Eyes

Long ago you told me of a song.
It made you cry, from vulnerability.
It made me cry, too, from joy and disbelief.
I played it like a broken record.

I remember what we were doing, how I was sitting, where we were going. I remember how I kissed you.

As I remember that moment,
I remember that joy.

So as much as I played it like a broken record,
I soon felt that way too.

CRUSH

Everything hurts.
Make it stop

Please.

Punch

I miss you

Three words that can hold more punch than a bowl at a party.

Thief

I guarded my most treasured piece under lock and key
He reached in faster than I could blink

When I looked down to see,
There lay in his hands, that part of me.

Thirty-Four Days

I was in a cafe in Melbourne
When I felt my whole body quiver, and my heart sink.
I immediately lost my appetite.

I tried to fight the tears
But it seemed that fighting them brought it on a lot stronger.
Count to three, deep breaths.

One …
        Two …
                Three.

A friend took my phone, held my hands
She was speaking but the words were a blur.
I could feel everyone's eyes on me as I turned my back to the room and tried another time to stop myself from losing control.

Maybe it was that your message just read:
    Hi, how are you?

And not: *This was a mistake.*

Maybe it was just that it took you thirty-four days.

I wondered what I would say back.

The fact that I shouldn't didn't even cross my mind.
Everyone was so sure that it would hurt me more, but it didn't feel like I could feel any worse than at that very moment.

It was like I was the thread on a sewing machine, every line was slowly pulling away, and I was trying to contain it.

I wanted to write to you, but I could feel myself unravelling.

Hours went by, then days.

BONES

It was too late.
I don't want to know that I hurt you, or if I did.

I never wrote to you, and I'm sorry.

But we could never have been friends.
You may not have been in love with me, but I was still in love with you.

Promises

You made me promise not to sell the ring you bought
Not to burn the book you made
Not to throw any memories away.

But you promised me many things.

If you wanted me to keep my promises,
Why didn't you keep yours?

Wonder

I wonder what would happen if we ran into each other after this much time apart.

From every day, for years to

...

I wonder if
Twelve months on
You saw me

Would you feel indifferent,
As distant,
Or feel a tear?

Or would it shatter you like fireworks
On the first of the year?

Grief

I lost you.
You were still alive

Though you may as well have been dead.

Pain

You found something new to love.

You found someone new.

Forever

You bought me a rose dipped in lacquer
And trimmed in gold

You told me it will last forever
Because that's how long you knew we would.

Forever

Now the only thing I'm certain of forever, is

How long that word will haunt me.

I'm Okay

How were they to know?
You kept a brave face when nothing felt right.

Just when you think you've got yourself together, you look up in the mirror and your brow line crinkles. You look away, but it's already too late.

Like the empathic, hopeful look of love from your mother, you broke your own heart.

Your breaths become shorter, and your tears flow. You close your eyes as your fingers tighten their grip on the sink. Your breathing is broken but you allow a slow, deep breath.

You don't want to, but you look up at your reflection again:
Bright red eyes with tear-stained cheeks.

Almost as if you thought you'd look different.

Your mouth opens to release a cry so loud
Not even your repetitive "I'm okay" can convince your body.

Keep your gaze, and know you just expelled one more bad day.

You're not okay.

But you will be.

Permanent

I do not want temporary
I do not want to share.

I want it to be mine
Just mine, and all for me.

Alone

I grab a handful of sand and feel it slip between my fingers.
I look at my palm.

For every grain of sand slipping between my fingers
I wonder how easy it is to feel that small
How easy it is to feel alone
To feel the weight of everything on your shoulders
To not know what to do.

I look up to the sky, filled with stars,
And my eyes fill up with tears.

I close my eyes and exhale in relief once one tear falls down
my cheek ... As I open my eyes, I feel the wind sway me.

When suddenly,
Everything stops.

SURVIVE

You can get through this.
I will get through this!

Peace

When I shattered, you left with my pieces.
When you left, you took my peace.

Time

There is no race
There is no competition.

You do not understand the depth of my emotions.
You may feel in black and white
Where I feel in colours

Do not tell me it will take this or that long
I will continue to take my time
As slow as first gear or as fast as fifth

I will eventually reach the finish line.

Relieved

I would put makeup on, do my hair
I wore that skirt you once lifted
With those boots that clinked with every step

I would smile, and laugh and drink
Only, every time the door would open
I would turn and be disappointed,
But relieved too
That it wasn't you

I couldn't understand why,
Although I was in a room full of people
I still searched for you.

Thanks for the Memory

I asked a stranger if his cologne was the one in the red bottle.
The one I used to smell whenever
I dug my head into your neck
You held my hand, standing upwind
I rolled over to your side of the bed.

Suddenly every memory flicked through my mind, like the turning pages of a book. I'm doing what I can to close it.

He interrupted my thoughts: "How did you know?"

I smiled, feeling every nerve in my lips pinch, trying that much harder to keep my lips that way.

BONES

The Little Things

I used to drink from two straws.
It was a little quirk of mine
And the only person who knew was you.

I had a broken heart when I got to know this girl.
She was beautiful and kind.
The kind of girl whose smile made you smile.
I became fond of her.

She once handed me a drink with two straws.

I remember the little things, and I start to cry.
But this isn't about me.
It's about the little things.

And out of all the little things,

She was definitely one.

Steam

The steam collected around the ceiling, hiding the mirrors.

I remembered when I left you a note in the mirror that one time and in the car window that other time. I remembered the smile on your face when you saw it, calling me cute, kissing me.

I felt as broken as the water splattering around me, spilling into the drain.

It felt like the pain wouldn't end.
And it didn't, for a long while.

Expired

I went to the supermarket and saw milk for half price.
I had a closer look,
The expiration date was the day after tomorrow.

I thought, when people know an end is coming
Or the best of it is over,

Is that why they use it up until it's empty?

Rock

You wondered if the words on your pages would burn me,
So you tried to light me afire.

But you cannot burn something that has already been burnt.
For when lava melts and lays itself along the sand,
It becomes rock.

So if I am now a rock, and you, paper,
Maybe I will set myself alight
Just to watch you burn.

You

If I was asked to keep only one memory
I wouldn't have a clue.

But if I could go anywhere …
It wouldn't be to a *where*, it would be to a *who*.

It would be to you.

The Pacific

As I see my location pulsing on the map, I find his.
Separated by the length of the Pacific Ocean.

My afternoon, his night ...
I drop my phone and watch the ripples in the water

I shiver
I remember the night when he whispered he will never forget
The curves of my body
My crooked smile
The colour of my eyes.

I dip my toes into the ocean and feel my body reanimate.
As far apart as we were, I wonder
How close we are to touch the same thing once more,
To feel the same from the other side of the ocean.

I know he felt the lengths ... and the depths too.

An ocean apart but I'm still learning how to swim.

Dear Diary

Today,
I forgot the sound of your voice.

REALISE

Welcome to the party,
Where you finally find your peace.

Thank You

Thank you

For the experience of something so magnificent
Something so powerful and beautiful
That not having it, placed me in agony
Enough to know that it was real
What I felt was real
What we had was real
Because it was the hardest thing I have ever had to experience.

But I want to thank you for breaking my heart
Because it showed me how strong I am,
What I am capable of.

One Day

It is sad that my greatest was not enough for one.
And although it will be, one day.

It is enough for me.

Heartbeat

Though my heart was hesitant,
Its beat, deafening like drums
You'll know when to let go,
When the time comes.

Reflection

Sometimes I reflect on specific moments we shared
It's part of my personal timeline with key milestones, like:
Ah, we were together for a year by that stage, or
That was just about two months after we broke up.

It used to be gloomier than it is now.

Now, I see myself reflect on you as a person whom I loved
whenever I recollect a memory from my past.

Either way, it cannot be erased or altered.
You changed me in many ways.
Sometimes, it even makes me smile.

I hope you're happy.

Symmetry

If there's anything that I have learnt,
It is that the pain in your chest reminds you, you're alive.

That as you feel so much suffering
You will one day feel solace.

For to know one, you must have known the other.

Arizona

Driving to Utah from Arizona
Destination: Monument Valley.
Speed up to 150 miles
She reminds me it's no rally.

In company, a bronzed beauty
Not alone with my musings.
I loved her, my best friend
We laughed, cried, and blasted music.

A vehicle full of thrills
Truly more than a delight.
Cactus and tumbleweed surround us
Not a soul left in sight.

Shed a tear, not out of fear
The road was open for my choosing.
Not wishing you were here
I smiled as we were cruising.

Looking back to this moment,
Must be one of my favourites.
I'm glad I shared it with her,
I'm glad I savoured it.

Wind

I read somewhere that you should be cautious about how hard you fall for another, because the depth of the fall is the magnitude of the pain.

But you cannot tame a heart that loves deeply
For it is in its freest, purest form.

I may fall hard, to the ground
But if it was not for the wind, forcing movement
Everything would lie stagnant.

So, I refuse to let this harden my heart, regardless how painful its end is. I just have to keep moving. Because love is anything but mediocre. Love is felt in the depths, and love is the very thing that will help me heal.

Wet

I love you.
Do not speak those words if you fail to feel them too.
Do you know the meaning of love?

I think love can be found in our worst moments.
Don't you?

Within the pain,
While my eyes are red, and my skin is flushed.
Love is when you remain by my side while I cry.

Love is when you pull me closer
Raise my chin
Wipe my cheek
Hold me gently, and whisper
I promise to only make you wet in other places.

Feel

Before you
I did not know that I was capable of feeling so deeply.

After you
I did not know that I was capable of feeling so deeply.

Knowing what I know now
I know that I am yet to experience more
More that I have not already felt yet.

Am I scared?
But how much more fulfilling is it when you give in and feel it crawl inside you, from the tips of your fingers to the ends of your toes?

Than to not feel at all?

CONQUER

Once you identify your power,
Nothing can stand against you.

Indifferent

Beginner's luck, thought I hit the jackpot with you.
Caught the bouquet at your mother's wedding.
Crossed my fingers that I'd take your last name.

Soon I learned superstitions are false.

So I dare you now:
Tell me to be careful with a mirror
And if it breaks, I will face years of bad luck.

I will shatter it to show you
What I have done means nothing.
I just simply no longer give a fuck.

Classic

An old car was parked in front of me
I kicked its tyre
Who would want this thing?
It's battered, rusty, the interior is worn, the seats are torn ...
It barely starts.

I caught my reflection in the window
A literal moment of reflection
Perhaps you could say I was describing it the way I viewed myself.

I've been hurt,
Looked my worst,
My insides might feel torn,
And sometimes it'll be hard to make that first step

But someone will always see past that,
See more than what you might
They'll want to help rebuild you
Into something they want to see you become.

A better version of yourself.
I smiled into my reflection,

That *someone* is me.

The Next

I will admit it: I am afraid
Too afraid to allow myself to love somebody else
Too afraid to allow anyone else the ability to break me again
So I will just love myself instead
Until I feel unbroken
And unbreakable.

BONES

Now

I had the best of you, and
I was the only one you showed your worst to.

Perhaps it seems unjust because
I cannot say you had the best of me.

The best of me will always be, here
Now.

Heavy

You would have said that I was the ball,
That the chain was around your neck.

But if it was, explain:
When the chain broke, why was it that I began to feel free?

BONES

1965

There was nothing but the sound of the waves kissing the shores and the engine's explosive exhaust. The taste of sea salt on my tongue and the air smelt of pines, leather and fuel.

The sun came down to meet with the raspberry-glazed, lilac skies. I wanted to experience it in all its unfiltered, raw beauty.

I pulled my sunglasses off and placed them in my lap. My eyes were burning but I didn't mind.

The engine heated the car like a hot summer's day, so I rolled the windows down and felt the wind through my hair.

My mind was running as fast as I was building speed.

We glided downhill, swerved around bends and I felt the power of the throttle as the car soared uphill.

It would shake and rattle whenever we came to a halt. I didn't always know where I wanted to go, but that was part of the beauty.

I just sought the thrill of an adventure.

Heads would turn, kids would point … but I was unaware.

It felt like a timeless fantasy. As if I was dozing on the sand under the sun, dreaming of a day this enchanting.

The moment itself was that intoxicating.
I never felt alone even when I was.

My foot heavy on the accelerator, stationary turned screeching
My very own pulse stimulator, speed limit, probable breaching.

Roll

Let it in.

Fill your eyes and swell them
Let the tears roll down your cheek.

It's okay.

You will feel like you're trying to roll uphill.
You will stop and start again, to roll backwards just a little.

It's okay.

Endure the pain, grieve your loss and feel.

Every time you get closer to the top, you fill your lungs with clearer air. Not far now.

When you reach midway, you will begin to see the beauty surrounding you, and all the flowers in bloom filling the horizon. You'll look back and find comfort in knowing how far you've made it on your own. Even if the top of this mountain is the bottom of the next, you will always persevere.

So let it *all in*.

You will move on. Away from broken twigs, dry branches and onto the mountain's towering peak,
Into a field full of colour.

I Wish

I wish it never happened.

The beauty of this statement is, if it didn't happen, you wouldn't be where you are right now. Your life, their life, the lives of everyone around you, would be very different. Every decision, no matter how minuscule, affects everyone.

When you wish something never happened, realise the impact that situation had on you. You're a different person because of that. It needed to happen for you to grow. For you to become who you will.

Quit allowing your past to hold you back to someone you used to be. Let go of the past. Let go of everything you wish never happened. It did. You can't change that. You have no power to. Don't regret it. Just move on. Move on and quit stunting your personal growth.

How

        I need your help. How did you do it?
Do what?

        How did you get over him?
        He was the love of your life!
I thought he was.

        You guys were perfect!
Nothing is.

        What was it like?
I feel like … it almost killed me.

        How did you do it?
How much of my time did I want to spend agonising?
I only realised that you lose time – you never get it back again.
That's why time is so valuable.

        Wait – but *how*?
I forced myself to feel everything.
I got mad, I cried, I screamed, I prayed, I cried more. I fought every part of me not to go back to something so bad for me just for a second of comfort.

        I find that part the most difficult.
This is temporary pain. It's not worth it when you realise the future you want, is dependent on this very moment.

        It doesn't feel temporary.
No, but it only lasts as long as it has done its job in building your character and strength. When it has taught you what you needed to learn. Why should you continue spending the most valuable thing, your time, on something that no longer holds any value?

Jesus Christ

I pray for peace, I pray for healing
His power like loving, lively light.
My pillowcases no longer catching tears
When I lay my head down each night.

Trigger

Pull the trigger, I'm unbothered
What's not meant for me, I'll release.

I'm no longer stuck where you left me
I've healed and found my peace.

The best part is, I didn't become you
My heart remained pure and kind.

I pray your heart is content, and
I pray that's what you'll find.

Developed

Sometimes after a while in the dark, you may feel you're still not ready. But sometimes, just like a train through a tunnel, you find your way out to the light eventually.

I finally developed that roll of film.

I've lived black and white, greyscale, sepia and full colour, and I am thankful for the spectrum.

EPILOGUE

After recollecting this time in my life, I vividly see how far I have come. I recognise the belief in myself to overcome my pain and find my inner peace. I recognise that, although I was heartbroken, I expressed my vulnerabilities fully unfiltered, in the hopes that it would aid not just my pain, but yours, too.

Regardless of the social constructs that attempt to limit you, allow yourself that same vulnerability and patience.

Just as we have all experienced pain, we all already carry peace. Don't leave your peace in the past, don't leave it with the person who broke you. Carry it with you wherever you go. Your peace is vital for your pain, because it is a part of your healing. You can find your peace by exposing the very thing that hurts, so express your pain through all your untold stories.

Although concealing your pain may seem easier, it's not. Hiding anything is bad, even secrets can make you sick. Hiding only allows you a waiting period. For someone to come and find you while you're silent and bent over in a corner behind thick walls. And when you finally get up or move, your body aches. But what if you hide yourself a little too well and no one finds you? Or what if you remain in hiding for so long you've accustomed yourself to the darkness?

The underlying question is, don't you want others to see you for who you truly are? I hope you will allow yourself that honour.

If where you are in your journey isn't serving you, leave. Get up, dust yourself off, and walk away. It may be hard. However, your pain is there to serve a purpose. It is necessary for progression, sometimes it is also necessary for knowledge. Just picture when you grazed your knee after falling off your bike as a child. I bet you went slower around that same bend the next time. See? Purpose.

BONES

I'm certain you have heard 'choose kindness, because you don't know what someone may be going through', and this book is quite a testament to that. However, I believe this kindness should be applied regardless of that mentality. Always choose kindness. Not because you must, or because someone else may be going through something, but because of *who you are*. This particularly applies to yourself. Just as you would treat a loved one with the care, love and patience you know they deserve, perhaps it's time you allow yourself that same kindness.

I hope wherever this finds you, this allows you a glimmer of hope. Because I can guarantee you, although it may not feel like it in this very moment, that glimmer will turn into a full-blown, blinding light. And it's okay if it doesn't feel like you're making progress, healing isn't linear.

Don't dwell on who you were in your past. Keep applauding yourself for becoming.

Be careful, though. If you continue to follow this path, you may end up reflecting on your past with admiration for your strength and reclamation of your peace, just as I have.

With love,

Janette x

@janettevoski

www.ingramcontent.com/pod-product-compliance
Lightning Source LLC
Chambersburg PA
CBHW020328010526
44107CB00054B/2026